The Archers Family Tree

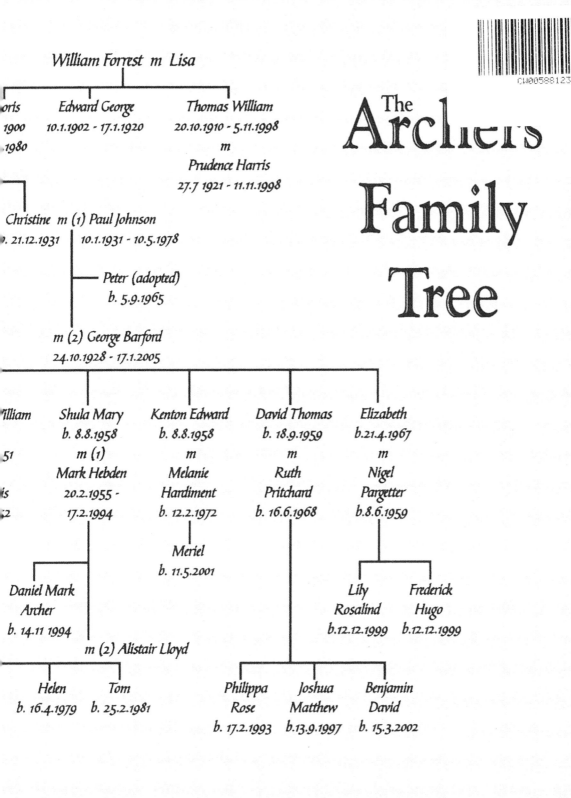

William Forrest m Lisa

oris
1900
1980

Edward George
10.1.1902 - 17.1.1920

Thomas William
20.10.1910 - 5.11.1998
m
Prudence Harris
27.7 1921 - 11.11.1998

Christine m (1) Paul Johnson
. 21.12.1931   10.1.1931 - 10.5.1978

Peter (adopted)
b. 5.9.1965

m (2) George Barford
24.10.1928 - 17.1.2005

'illiam
51
is
2

Shula Mary
b. 8.8.1958
m (1)
Mark Hebden
20.2.1955 -
17.2.1994

Kenton Edward
b. 8.8.1958
m
Melanie
Hardiment
b. 12.2.1972

Meriel
b. 11.5.2001

David Thomas
b. 18.9.1959
m
Ruth
Pritchard
b. 16.6.1968

Elizabeth
b.21.4.1967
m
Nigel
Pargetter
b.8.6.1959

Daniel Mark
Archer
b. 14.11 1994

Lily
Rosalind
b.12.12.1999

Frederick
Hugo
b.12.12.1999

m (2) Alistair Lloyd

Helen
b. 16.4.1979

Tom
b. 25.2.1981

Philippa
Rose
b. 17.2.1993

Joshua
Matthew
b.13.9.1997

Benjamin
David
b. 15.3.2002

DIARY 2008
The Archers

F

FRANCES LINCOLN LIMITED

PUBLISHERS

Frances Lincoln Limited
4 Torriano Mews
Torriano Avenue
London NW5 2RZ
www.franceslincoln.com

The Archers Diary 2008

Astronomical information reproduced, with permission, from data
supplied by HM Nautical Almanac Office, copyright © Council for
the Central Laboratory of the Research Councils.

British Library cataloguing-in-publication data
A catalogue record for this book is available from
the British Library

ISBN: 978-0-7112-2778-1

Printed in China

First Frances Lincoln edition 2007

ACKNOWLEDGEMENTS

The Publisher would like to thank Vanessa Whitburn, Editor of
The Archers, and Kate Oates, Producer, for their contribution.
Thanks also to Kate Tanner, Archers Addict Vicky Griffiths and
Kathy Brookes of Countryside Art for permission to use her
Archers Family Tree design.

ARCHERS ADDICTS

Archers Addicts is the Official Fan Club for BBC Radio 4's The
Archers. For further details and a colour brochure, please contact
PO Box 1951, Stratford-upon-Avon, Warwickshire, CV37 1YH
Telephone: 01789 20747
www.archers-addicts.com

Jacket: THE OLD BULL, INKBERROW, WORCESTERSHIRE
(photograph by Leon Tanner)

Below: DAN AND DORIS ARCHER (MONTE CRICK AND
GWEN BERRYMAN)

CALENDAR 2008

JANUARY
M	T	W	T	F	S	S
	1	2	3	4	5	6
7	8	9	10	11	12	13
14	15	16	17	18	19	20
21	22	23	24	25	26	27
28	29	30	31			

FEBRUARY
M	T	W	T	F	S	S
				1	2	3
4	5	6	7	8	9	10
11	12	13	14	15	16	17
18	19	20	21	22	23	24
25	26	27	28	29		

MARCH
M	T	W	T	F	S	S
					1	2
3	4	5	6	7	8	9
10	11	12	13	14	15	16
17	18	19	20	21	22	23
24	25	26	27	28	29	30
31						

APRIL
M	T	W	T	F	S	S
	1	2	3	4	5	6
7	8	9	10	11	12	13
14	15	16	17	18	19	20
21	22	23	24	25	26	27
28	29	30				

MAY
M	T	W	T	F	S	S
			1	2	3	4
5	6	7	8	9	10	11
12	13	14	15	16	17	18
19	20	21	22	23	24	25
26	27	28	29	30	31	

JUNE
M	T	W	T	F	S	S
						1
2	3	4	5	6	7	8
9	10	11	12	13	14	15
16	17	18	19	20	21	22
23	24	25	26	27	28	29
30						

JULY
M	T	W	T	F	S	S
	1	2	3	4	5	6
7	8	9	10	11	12	13
14	15	16	17	18	19	20
21	22	23	24	25	26	27
28	29	30	31			

AUGUST
M	T	W	T	F	S	S
				1	2	3
4	5	6	7	8	9	10
11	12	13	14	15	16	17
18	19	20	21	22	23	24
25	26	27	28	29	30	31

SEPTEMBER
M	T	W	T	F	S	S
1	2	3	4	5	6	7
8	9	10	11	12	13	14
15	16	17	18	19	20	21
22	23	24	25	26	27	28
29	30					

OCTOBER
M	T	W	T	F	S	S
		1	2	3	4	5
6	7	8	9	10	11	12
13	14	15	16	17	18	19
20	21	22	23	24	25	26
27	28	29	30	31		

NOVEMBER
M	T	W	T	F	S	S
					1	2
3	4	5	6	7	8	9
10	11	12	13	14	15	16
17	18	19	20	21	22	23
24	25	26	27	28	29	30

DECEMBER
M	T	W	T	F	S	S
1	2	3	4	5	6	7
8	9	10	11	12	13	14
15	16	17	18	19	20	21
22	23	24	25	26	27	28
29	30	31				

CALENDAR 2009

JANUARY
M	T	W	T	F	S	S
			1	2	3	4
5	6	7	8	9	10	11
12	13	14	15	16	17	18
19	20	21	22	23	24	25
26	27	28	29	30	31	

FEBRUARY
M	T	W	T	F	S	S
						1
2	3	4	5	6	7	8
9	10	11	12	13	14	15
16	17	18	19	20	21	22
23	24	25	26	27	28	

MARCH
M	T	W	T	F	S	S
						1
2	3	4	5	6	7	8
9	10	11	12	13	14	15
16	17	18	19	20	21	22
23	24	25	26	27	28	29
30	31					

APRIL
M	T	W	T	F	S	S
		1	2	3	4	5
6	7	8	9	10	11	12
13	14	15	16	17	18	19
20	21	22	23	24	25	26
27	28	29	30			

MAY
M	T	W	T	F	S	S
				1	2	3
4	5	6	7	8	9	10
11	12	13	14	15	16	17
18	19	20	21	22	23	24
25	26	27	28	29	30	31

JUNE
M	T	W	T	F	S	S
1	2	3	4	5	6	7
8	9	10	11	12	13	14
15	16	17	18	19	20	21
22	23	24	25	26	27	28
29	30					

JULY
M	T	W	T	F	S	S
		1	2	3	4	5
6	7	8	9	10	11	12
13	14	15	16	17	18	19
20	21	22	23	24	25	26
27	28	29	30	31		

AUGUST
M	T	W	T	F	S	S
					1	2
3	4	5	6	7	8	9
10	11	12	13	14	15	16
17	18	19	20	21	22	23
24	25	26	27	28	29	30
31						

SEPTEMBER
M	T	W	T	F	S	S
	1	2	3	4	5	6
7	8	9	10	11	12	13
14	15	16	17	18	19	20
21	22	23	24	25	26	27
28	29	30				

OCTOBER
M	T	W	T	F	S	S
			1	2	3	4
5	6	7	8	9	10	11
12	13	14	15	16	17	18
19	20	21	22	23	24	25
26	27	28	29	30	31	

NOVEMBER
M	T	W	T	F	S	S
						1
2	3	4	5	6	7	8
9	10	11	12	13	14	15
16	17	18	19	20	21	22
23	24	25	26	27	28	29
30						

DECEMBER
M	T	W	T	F	S	S
	1	2	3	4	5	6
7	8	9	10	11	12	13
14	15	16	17	18	19	20
21	22	23	24	25	26	27
28	29	30	31			

GILES PARK

INTRODUCTION

The Archers is a story about country people struggling, as we all do, to make sense of the world they live in. Add a dash of nostalgia, a sprinkling of laughter and the occasional tear, and it is easy to understand why, for some people, listening to *The Archers* is an essential part of their daily routine. For them *The Archers Diary* contains a wealth of fun and information.

Within these pages we find beautiful pictures of the English countryside reflecting the rich farming environment familiar to the families of Ambridge. Some pictures remind us of storylines – such as Lynda's llamas, the notorious peacock at The Bull, Eccles, and the even more notorious Grundy ferrets! The history of *The Archers* is touched upon, with vintage pictures of the cast and the dates of landmark occasions: at the same time we see the cast in studio, scripts in hand, and we realise that this is still, and gloriously, a radio programme. For that reason there are as many versions of Ambridge as there are listeners!

We hope you have as much pleasure in using your *Archers Diary* as we have had in putting it together. Please let us know your thoughts and ideas about what you would like to see in future Archers Diaries. They are for you, without whom there would be no programme.

Archers Addicts
Official fan club for BBC Radio 4's *The Archers*
www.archers-addicts.com

Harold Rodge (Bumpy)   *April 11/4/60.*

DAN ARCHER

Harry Oakes

Harry Oakes

DORIS ARCHER

Gwen Berryman

Gwen Berryman

PHILIP ARCHER

Norman Painting

WALTER GABRIEL

Chris Gittins

Chris Gittins.

MRS. PERKINS

Pauline Seville

TOM FORREST

Bob Arnold

Best of Luck Bob Arnold

JOHN TREGORRAN

Basil Jones

Basil Jones

CAROL GREY

Anne Cullen

Noreen Richards *Anne Cullen.*

NED LARKIN

Bill Payne

Bill Payne

June Spencer
(Rita Flynn)

JILL ARCHER

Patricia Greene

JACK ARCHER

Denis Folwell

Denis Folwell [signature]

PEGGY ARCHER

Thelma Rogers

PRU FORREST

Mary Dalley

Best Wishes
Mary Dalley [signature]

PAUL JOHNSON

Leslie Dunn

Leslie Dunn [signature]

CHRISTINE JOHNSON

Lesley Saweard

Best Wishes
Lesley Saweard [signature]

JIMMY GRANGE

Alan Rothwell

[signature]

MR. GRENVILLE

Michael Shaw

Michael Shaw [signature]

PRODUCER

Tony Shryane

Valma Hodgetts [signature]

Tony Shryane [signature]

BIRTHDAYS AND ANNIVERSARIES

You can record whether or not you share special dates with those in Ambridge, as well as Archers gift ideas so that you are not stuck for inspiration when the time comes.

JANUARY ....

....

....

....

....

....

FEBRUARY ....

....

....

....

....

....

MARCH ....

....

....

....

....

....

APRIL ....

....

....

....

....

....

MAY ....

....

....

....

....

....

JUNE ....

....

....

....

....

....

JULY

OCTOBER

AUGUST

NOVEMBER

SEPTEMBER

DECEMBER

CHRISTMAS

THE ULTIMATE CONTACT SHEET

FAMILY

Name	Name	Name	Name ....
H	H	H	H ....
W..	W..	W..	W..
M	M	M	M ....

Name	Name	Name	Name ....
H	H	H	H ....
W..	W..	W..	W..
M	M	M	M ....

WORK CONTACTS

....	....	....	....
....	....	....	....
....	....	....	....

NEIGHBOURS / DOCTOR / DENTIST

NEIGHBOURS		DOCTOR	DENTIST
....	....	....	....
....	....	....	....
....	....	....	....

OPTICIAN / HOSPITAL / POLICE STATION / LOCAL COUNCIL

OPTICIAN	HOSPITAL	POLICE STATION	LOCAL COUNCIL
....	....	....	....
....	....	....	....
....	....	....	....

BANKS

....
....
....

BUILDING SOCIETIES

MORTGAGE LENDER/LANDLORD

....
....
....

FAVOURITE RESTAURANTS/TAKEAWAYS

....
....
....

OTHER USEFUL NUMBERS

BRAIN OF BORSETSHIRE?

How big an Archers fan are you? *You listen to* The Archers *every night and you think you know all about Ambridge and its inhabitants. Now's your chance to find out whether or not* **you** *are the brain of Borsetshire! The Quiz is in four sections. You'll find the answers upside down at the bottom of the page. When you've finished mark your answers and check your rating. You could be in for a surprise …*

CATCH THE CHARACTER!

1 Caroline Sterling has invited you to a party, what drinks does she provide?

a) That nectar beloved of the gods (and Grundys) – cider!

b) A ruby vintage Port to go with a fragrant cheese

c) Freshly squeezed orange juice. The Sterlings are well known teetotallers

2 You need to visit Brian Aldridge. What vehicle would most impress him?

a) A red Mercedes convertible: matches your feminine charms

b) A horse and trap: the only way to travel and environmentally friendly too!

c) A shiny 4x4: robust yet flashy, the perfect combination!

3 Lynda Snell is coming round for supper. What's on the menu?

a) She thinks she's classy so *Soufflé au Fromage (avec courgettes provençales)* – *bon appetit!*

b) She's conventional so a roast beef and Yorkshire pudding with apple crumble to follow

c) She's no food snob so good old fish and chips with a slice of bread and butter

4 Which cartoon character does David Archer most resemble?

a) Homer Simpson: good natured, a couch potato and very slow on the uptake

b) Popeye: muscular, eats his spinach, and fights off all foes

c) SpongeBob SquarePants: hard-worker, great cook and very absorbent

5 If Helen Archer were a cheese which one would she be?

a) Montgomery cheddar – tasty, flavoursome and a little nutty

b) Somerset Brie – oozing elegance and decadence, with a soft gooey centre

c) Borsetshire Blue – sharp, salty and worth a second bite

AMBRIDGE ALLSORTS

1 Ambridge is a seething hotbed of scandal. Who did Brian have an affair with?

a) Betty Tucker, because he was sorry for her when Jennifer told her off for putting the fish knives in the dishwasher

b) Siobhan Hathaway, because he liked her style and she spoke Hungarian

c) Mandy Beesborough, because she knew how to keep quiet

② Which celebrity played Nelson Gabriel's upper class girlfriend, Penelope Radford, in 1980?
a) Anneka Rice, who challenged Nelson to help her re-decorate the Village Hall
b) Angela Rippon – taking a break from reading the Nine O' Clock News on BBC1
c) The Duchess of Kent, so that the accent would be truly authentic

③ What was the name of the horse Grace Archer saved from the Grey Gables stable fire?
a) Midnight
b) Starlight
c) Sunlight

④ Who was the last actor to play Dan Archer?
a) Harry Oakes
b) Monte Crick
c) Frank Middlemass

⑤ In what year was Lynda Snell born?
a) She sounds young and sweet, 1957
b) She's had the big one…1947
c) She's been directing Ambridge dramatics for years – 1927

PUT THEM IN THEIR PLACE!

- Where do David and Ruth Archer live?
- Which farm went organic in 1984?
- The Sterlings currently own Grange Farm. Name the previous occupants?
- Who used to live at Nightingale Farm before retiring to The Laurels?
- Which farmer installed a solar-heated swimming pool in the garden?

NEIGHBOURS? FRIENDS OR FOE!

- Emma Carter married a Grundy – which one?
- Tom Archer trashed the GM crops belonging to which Ambridge farmer?
- Clive Horrobin set fire to the Old Police House in 2004. Who was living there at the time?
- Who was part of a racist gang who targeted Usha Gupta in the 1990s?
- Someone came between David and Ruth Archer in 2006. What was his name?

HOW DID YOU SCORE?

16–20 You know more about Ambridge than Phil does! Give yourself a pat on the back and a glass of champagne.

11–15 Excellent work – you are obviously a loyal fan and could make regular contributions to Jennifer Aldridge's web site …

6–10 A good effort but you have a long way to go before you become the brain of Borsetshire! Perhaps you could enrol for a local history course at Borchester College …

0–5 Bottom of the class with Eddie Grundy. You need to swot up on your Archers trivia over a pint or two of Shires.

AMBRIDGE ALLSORTS

1. (b) Brian had an affair with Siobhan Hathaway that resulted in the birth of his son Ruairi
2. (b) Angela Rippon played Nelson's upper class girlfriend, Penelope Radford
3. (a) The horse was called Midnight and belonged to Grace's sister-in-law, Christine Archer
4. (c) Harry Oakes, Monte Crick, Edgar Harrison have all played Dan but Frank Middlemass was the last actor to do so, until Dan's death in 1986
5. (b) Lynda Snell was born on 29 May 1947

CATCH THE CHARACTER!

1. (b) Caroline will certainly offer the cheese and knows that Port is the perfect accompaniment
2. (a) Although you can give yourself a point if you chose (c), Brian could never resist a pretty woman driving a red Mercedes convertible!
3. (a) Soufflé au Fromage is the perfect choice, and she'll so love to be able to tell you why her recipe for courgettes provençales is better than yours!
4. (b) David resembles Popeye – when he's not rescuing cattle and fighting off Ruth's would-be suitors he's tearing down tree houses
5. (c) Helen is definitely the Borsetshire Blue … for a start she created it!

BRIDGE FARM

Farm Facts

Bridge Farm comprises 140 acres rented from Borchester Land, with an additional 32 acres from other landlords.

ACRES PER CROP:
- 115 grassland
- 20 barley
- 15 wheat
- 6 potatoes
- 4 carrots
- 2 leeks
- 3 swedes
- 2 Dutch cabbage
- 4 mixed vegetable and salad

STOCK:
- 290 Friesians
- 45 heifers/calves

Tenant farmers, Tony and Pat Archer, anticipated the popularity of organic food, deciding to go organic in 1984. They produce a variety of vegetables for sale at Ambridge Organics, their shop in Borchester. Pat's carrots have even made it into the supermarkets, proudly boasting a specially commissioned Bridge Farm label. Bridge Farm is also famous for its delicious homemade yoghurt and ice-cream, and Helen's Borsetshire Blue cheese is much enjoyed, if only by the locals. It's been hard work and Tony's endless moaning hasn't made life any easier. However, Pat has risen to the challenge and, somewhat surprisingly, they are still together!

- Not one to be curbed by convention, Pat proposed to Tony, who was engaged to Mary Weston when first they met.

- Louiza Patikas is the third actor to play Helen. Frances Graham and Bonnie Engstrom both played the part previously.

Sizzling Storylines

- Who can forget the death of Pat and Tony's eldest son, John, on Tom's seventeenth birthday? A tear wet the eye of many a listener as Tony lamented the discovery of his son crushed underneath his Ferguson tractor.

- Life hasn't been easy for entrepreneur Tom and his 'sizzling' sausages; his business went under in 2005 but, not one to give in easily, he resumed production with a little help from Uncle Brian.

- It's not all neighbourly love in Ambridge and, in 1999, Tom was charged for deliberately damaging GM rape crops at Home Farm.

- What could be more dramatic than the tragic demise of Helen's boyfriend Greg, at his own hands? Followed by Helen's ongoing struggle with a food disorder. . .

DECEMBER | JANUARY

WEEK 1
2008

31 Monday

New Year's Eve
Last Quarter

1 Tuesday

New Year's Day
Holiday, UK, Republic of Ireland, Canada, USA, Australia and New Zealand
JACK AND PEGGY WOOLLEY MARRIED 1991
THE ARCHERS FIRST BROADCAST NATIONWIDE 1951

2 Wednesday

Holiday, Scotland and New Zealand

3 Thursday

4 Friday

5 Saturday

6 Sunday

Epiphany

PHIL ARCHER (NORMAN PAINTING)

7 Monday

JENNIFER ALDRIDGE BORN 1945

8 Tuesday

New Moon

9 Wednesday

10 Thursday

Islamic New Year (subject to sighting of the moon)
PAT ARCHER BORN 1952

11 Friday

12 Saturday

13 Sunday

JANUARY

14 Monday

15 Tuesday

First Quarter

16 Wednesday

17 Thursday

GEORGE BARFORD DIED 2005

18 Friday

19 Saturday

NOLUTHANDO MADIKANE BORN 2001

20 Sunday

MIKE KELLY

JANUARY

21 Monday

Holiday, USA (Martin Luther King's birthday)
BRENDA TUCKER BORN 1981

22 Tuesday

Full Moon

23 Wednesday

24 Thursday

25 Friday

26 Saturday

27 Sunday

BRENDA TUCKER (AMY SHINDLER) AND TOM ARCHER (TOM GRAHAM)

28 Monday   Holiday, Australia (Australia Day)

29 Tuesday

30 Wednesday   *Last Quarter*
KATHY PERKS BORN 1953

31 Thursday

1 Friday

2 Saturday   ROY TUCKER BORN 1978

3 Sunday

4 Monday

TIM HATHAWAY BORN 1960

5 Tuesday

Shrove Tuesday

6 Wednesday

Ash Wednesday
Holiday, New Zealand (Waitangi Day)

7 Thursday

Chinese New Year
New Moon

8 Friday

9 Saturday

WILLIAM GRUNDY BORN 1983

10 Sunday

FEBRUARY

11 Monday

12 Tuesday

Holiday, USA (Lincoln's birthday)

13 Wednesday

14 Thursday

St Valentine's Day
First Quarter

15 Friday

16 Saturday

TONY ARCHER BORN 1951

17 Sunday

PHILIPPA ARCHER BORN 1993
MARK HEBDEN DIED 1994

18 Monday   Holiday, USA (Washington's birthday)

19 Tuesday

20 Wednesday   MARK HEBDEN BORN 1955

21 Thursday   *Full Moon*

22 Friday

23 Saturday

24 Sunday

TOM FORREST (BOB ARNOLD)

25 Monday

TOM ARCHER BORN 1981
NEIL AND SUSAN CARTER MARRIED 1984
JOHN ARCHER DIED 1998

26 Tuesday

27 Wednesday

28 Thursday

29 Friday

Last Quarter

1 Saturday

St David's Day
CHRISTINE AND GEORGE BARFORD MARRIED 1979

2 Sunday

Mothering Sunday, UK

BRIDGE FARM

PERFECT PORK

Pat takes great pride in Tom and supports his business whenever she can, even though she would have preferred him to remain at Bridge Farm rather than work for Brian Aldridge. She's come up with all sorts of pork recipes over the years, and this is one of her tastiest dishes.

Serves 4

INGREDIENTS

4 Gloucester Old Spot lean chops
   (other pork will do!)
4 tablespoons seasoned flour
14g ($1/_2$oz) dripping
4 onions, peeled and chopped
2 green peppers, deseeded and chopped
1 x 400g (15oz) tin chopped tomatoes
Juice $1/_2$ lemon
1 level tablespoon dark soy sauce
1 level dessertspoon sugar
1 tablespoon tomato purée
300ml (10fl oz) chicken stock

METHOD

- Trim the fat from the chops and dip both sides in the seasoned flour. Putting the flour in a large freezer bag makes this quick and easy with much less mess!
- Brown both sides quickly and place in a lidded casserole dish.
- Gently fry the onions and chopped peppers for 5 minutes until the onions are soft.
- Stir in all the remaining ingredients and bring to the boil, then pour over the chops.
- Cook in the oven for 1 hour at gas mark 4 (180C/350F).

PAT'S TOP TIP

Delicious served with a generous dish of mashed potato, and of course organic carrots tossed in butter and flat-leaved parsley!

MARCH

3 Monday

4 Tuesday

5 Wednesday

6 Thursday

7 Friday   *New Moon*

8 Saturday

9 Sunday

10 Monday   Commonwealth Day

11 Tuesday

12 Wednesday

13 Thursday

14 Friday   *First Quarter*

15 Saturday   EDDIE GRUNDY BORN 1951
BENJAMIN ARCHER BORN 2002

16 Sunday   Palm Sunday

EDWARD GRUNDY (BARRY FARRIMOND)

17 Monday

St Patrick's Day
Holiday, Northern Ireland and Republic of Ireland

18 Tuesday

NEWS OF NELSON GABRIEL'S DEATH 2001

19 Wednesday

20 Thursday

Maundy Thursday
Vernal Equinox

21 Friday

Good Friday
Holiday, UK, Canada, USA,
Australia and New Zealand
Full Moon

22 Saturday

23 Sunday

Easter Sunday

MARCH

24 Monday

Easter Monday
Holiday, UK (exc. Scotland), Republic of Ireland,
Canada, Australia and New Zealand

25 Tuesday

26 Wednesday

27 Thursday

28 Friday

29 Saturday

Last Quarter

30 Sunday

British Summertime begins
JAMES BELLAMY BORN 1973

GRANGE FARM

Grange Farm is a 50-acre dairy farm with a small herd of Guernseys supplying Mike Tucker's milk round

Before moving to Ambridge, Oliver Sterling ran a large farm in North Borsetshire, and was more than ready to rebuild the much loved but rapidly deteriorating Grange Farm. The farm had fallen into rack and ruin under the stewardship of the Grundys and, when they went bankrupt, the majority of the acreage was returned to Borchester Land. Fortunately Oliver had enough funds to buy and renovate the farm-house. He also purchased 50 acres to farm, more as a hobby than to make a living. He's married to Caroline, owner of Grey Gables, and over the years they have fostered a number of youngsters including Bruno and Carly, and assisting their troubled herdsman, Ed – looking after cows can be great therapy!

- Caroline has had an inexplicable run of bad luck with pets: Mike Tucker shot Charlie, her sweet little sheepdog puppy; Jack's bull terrier, Captain, died under her care; Ippy, her favourite horse, was stolen and another of her horses, Moonlight, was slashed by the vengeful Clive Horrobin!

- When Grange Farm herd became infected with brucellosis in 1978, a despondent Joe Grundy turned to drink. However, Eddie rose to the challenge and took up farming full-time . . . still went bankrupt though!

- Transfixed by jealousy, and eager to display his love for Clarrie, Eddie got a tattoo of a heart with 'Eddie and Clarrie' written underneath. Needless to say Clarrie was unimpressed; however the couple celebrated their silver wedding anniversary in 2006, so Eddie must be doing something right.

 ## Sizzling Storylines

- How could we forget the drama of that fateful night when Mark Hebden swerved his car to save Caroline's life, losing his own in the process?

- The Grundy's bankruptcy was a devastating moment in the history of Ambridge's farms. Despite Eddie's entrepreneurial endeavours and hard physical labour, he was forced to admit defeat after a long series of financial setbacks. Notification of bankruptcy came in January 2000, and the family were evicted by April.

- Not content with their small holdings, Oliver and Caroline scraped together the funds to buy Grey Gables in 2006. It was a battle with a few casualties along the way – Jolene was particularly perturbed when Caroline sold her share in The Bull to Lilian Bellamy – but eventually they got their prize, and the blessing of proprietor Jack Woolley.

MARCH | APRIL

31 Monday

1 Tuesday

2 Wednesday

GRACE ARCHER BORN 1929

3 Thursday

CAROLINE STERLING BORN 1955

4 Friday

5 Saturday

ROBERT SNELL BORN 1943

6 Sunday

New Moon

APRIL

7 Monday

GEORGE EDWARD GRUNDY BORN 2005

8 Tuesday

9 Wednesday

10 Thursday

11 Friday

PHIL AND GRACE ARCHER MARRIED 1955

12 Saturday

First Quarter
GUY PEMBERTON DIED 1996
KATE AND LUCAS MADIKANE MARRIED 2001
FIRST SUNDAY EPISODE 1998

13 Sunday

APRIL

---

14 Monday

---

15 Tuesday

---

16 Wednesday   HELEN ARCHER BORN 1979

---

17 Thursday

---

18 Friday

---

19 Saturday   OMNIBUS LENGTHENED TO 1HR 15MINS 1998

---

20 Sunday   Passover (Pesach), First Day
Full Moon

---

21 Monday

Birthday of Queen Elizabeth II
ELIZABETH PARGETTER BORN 1967

22 Tuesday

23 Wednesday

St George's Day
PHIL ARCHER BORN 1928
DAN ARCHER DIED 1986

24 Thursday

KATHY AND SID PERKS MARRIED 1987

25 Friday

Holiday, Australia and New Zealand (Anzac Day)

26 Saturday

Passover (Pesach), Seventh Day

27 Sunday

Passover (Pesach), Eighth Day

DAN ARCHER (EDGAR HARRISON) AND LILIAN ARCHER (ELIZABETH MARLOWE)

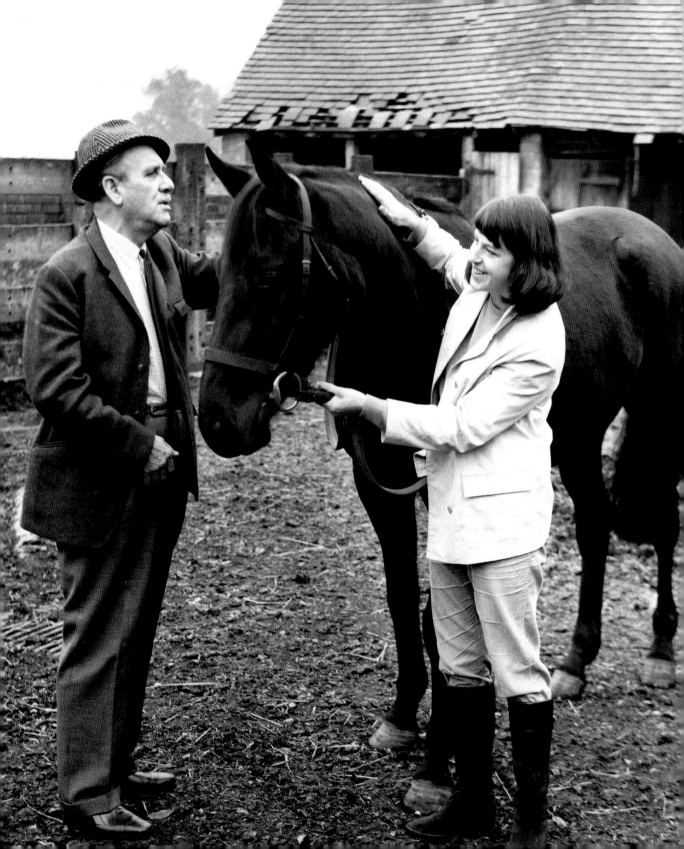

APRIL | MAY

28 Monday

Last Quarter
GERALD PARGETTER DIED 1988

29 Tuesday

30 Wednesday

1 Thursday

Ascension Day

2 Friday

3 Saturday

4 Sunday

5 Monday

Early May Bank Holiday, UK and Republic of Ireland
New Moon

6 Tuesday

7 Wednesday

HAYLEY AND ROY TUCKER MARRIED 2001
GREG TURNER DIED 2004

8 Thursday

9 Friday

10 Saturday

11 Sunday

Whit Sunday (Pentecost)
Mother's Day, Canada, USA, Australia and New Zealand
MERIEL ARCHER BORN 2001

MAY

12 Monday

13 Tuesday

14 Wednesday

FIVE TRIAL EPISODES RECORDED 1950

15 Thursday

16 Friday

17 Saturday

18 Sunday

Trinity Sunday

19 Monday

Holiday, Canada (Victoria Day)

20 Tuesday

Full Moon

21 Wednesday

22 Thursday

Corpus Christi
NEIL CARTER BORN 1957

23 Friday

24 Saturday

25 Sunday

THE ALDRIDGE FAMILY (from left to right) DEBBIE (TAMSIN GREIG), BRIAN (CHARLES COLLINGWOOD),
ADAM (ANDREW WINCOTT), JENNIFER (ANGELA PIPER), ALICE (HOLLIE CHAPMAN)

GILES PARK

GRANGE FARM

POTS AU CHOCOLAT

Clarrie may bake the best chocolate cake in Ambridge, but Caroline's *Pots au Chocolat* are unforgettable, even pleasing Joe Grundy when he's lucky enough to taste one. Creamy, dark and delicious, they combine Caroline's touch of class with fresh cream from Oliver's Guernseys to make the perfect dessert.

Serves 6

INGREDIENTS

1 packet ratafia biscuits
2 tablespoons brandy
170g (6oz) dark chocolate
300ml (10fl oz) Guernsey★ double cream
4 separated eggs
50g (2oz) Guernsey★ butter

★ or other cream and butter as available

METHOD

- Soak the ratafia biscuits in brandy.
- Melt the chocolate and butter in a *bain marie*.
- Beat in the egg yolks and allow to cool a little.
- Whisk the egg whites and fold in the whipped cream and melted chocolate.
- Take 6 ramekins and layer the bottom of each with the ratafia biscuits and cover with the chocolate mix.
- Chill for two hours before serving.

CAROLINE'S TOP TIP

For an almond flavour, substitute the ratafia biscuits with amaretti and sprinkle with toasted almonds.

26 Monday

Spring Bank Holiday, UK
Holiday, USA (Memorial Day)
JULIA AND LEWIS CARMICHAEL MARRIED 2005

27 Tuesday

28 Wednesday

Last Quarter
LYNDA SNELL BORN 1947

29 Thursday

JENNIFER AND BRIAN ALDRIDGE MARRIED 1976
THE ARCHERS FIRST BROADCAST IN MIDLAND REGION 1950

30 Friday

31 Saturday

1 Sunday

JUNE

2 Monday

Holiday, Republic of Ireland
Holiday, New Zealand (The Queen's birthday)

3 Tuesday

New Moon

4 Wednesday

5 Thursday

6 Friday

7 Saturday

8 Sunday

NIGEL PARGETTER BORN 1959
THE ARCHERS FIRST BROADCAST IN STEREO 1992

JOE GRUNDY (EDWARD KELSEY)

9 Monday

Jewish Feast of Weeks (Shavuot)
SID PERKS BORN 1944

10 Tuesday

First Quarter

11 Wednesday

12 Thursday

13 Friday

SIOBHAN HATHAWAY BORN 1965

14 Saturday

The Queen's official birthday (subject to confirmation)

15 Sunday

Father's Day, UK, Canada and USA

16 Monday

RUTH ARCHER BORN 1968

17 Tuesday

18 Wednesday

Full Moon

19 Thursday

FALLON ROGERS BORN 1985

20 Friday

Summer Solstice

21 Saturday

22 Sunday

ADAM MACY BORN 1967
CHRISTOPHER CARTER BORN 1988

JUNE

23 Monday

24 Tuesday

25 Wednesday

26 Thursday   *Last Quarter*

27 Friday

28 Saturday   PHOEBE ALDRIDGE BORN 1998

29 Sunday   CAROLINE AND OLIVER STERLING MARRIED 2006

BROOKFIELD FARM

Farm Facts

Brookfield is a 469-acre mixed farm incorporating the old holdings of Marney's and Hollowtree. Brookfield lamb is marketed co-operatively under the Hassett-Hills brand.

ACRES PER CROP:
- 312 grassland
- 80 cereals
- 15 oilseed rape
- 15 potatoes
- 12 beans
- 10 fodder beet
- 17 forage maize
- 8 set-aside

STOCK:
- 200 Friesians
- 80 heifers/calves
- 90 Herefords
- 300 ewes
- hens

David and Ruth Archer are the lynch pin of the Ambridge community, living at Brookfield with children Pip, Josh, Ben, and sheepdog Biff. Ruth's predecessors, Doris and Jill, always had time to put the kettle on, sit down and have a chat. Ruth, however, has broken the mould and is a fully qualified farmer in her own right. It took a while for her to convince David that women had as much to contribute on the farm as men, but now Ruth and David manage Brookfield together. They still rely on Phil for relief work, and on Jill to maintain the hens and bees ... running Brookfield is a real family affair.

- *The Archers of Wimberton Farm* (later to become Brookfield), was piloted on the Home Service, Midlands region, in May 1950.

- Sue Lawley got 20 million listeners for Desert Island Discs in 2001 when Norman Painting, who plays Phil Archer, was her guest.

- Timothy Bentinck, who plays David Archer, is the 12th Earl of Portland.

- In 1955 *The Archers* stole the launch-night thunder of ITV when Grace Archer, wife of Phil, was killed in a barn fire trying to rescue her horse. Her death drew an audience of 9.4m.

Anniversary Cliff-hangers

- There was joyous news in the 12,000th episode when Ruth announced her second pregnancy . . .

- . . . but sad news when she told her family she had cancer in the 13,000th episode

- In the 15,000th episode, Ruth risked her life with David and Brookfield for the sake of a night with with hunky herdsman, Sam Batton. Fortunately she resisted temptation!

 ## Sizzling Storylines

- The Brookfield Inheritance! This raged for months as the entire Archer clan rose up in arms to claim what they felt was rightfully theirs.

- When the farm expanded in 1997 the new cattle brought TB to the farm and infected cattle had to be slaughtered.

- During the foot-and-mouth crisis David quarantined the farm, even banning his children from Brookfield for fear the disease might spread to his precious herd which, thanks to his pre-emptive action, remained unscathed.

- Although Ruth had a risqué moment with Sam, David's also had a busy love life. On a return visit to Ambridge in 2006, ex-fiancé Sophie Barlow even stole a kiss and threatened to break the peace at Brookfield.

JUNE | JULY

30 Monday

1 Tuesday

Holiday, Canada (Canada Day)

2 Wednesday

3 Thursday

New Moon

4 Friday

Holiday, USA (Independence Day)
JOLENE AND SID PERKS MARRIED 2002

5 Saturday

6 Sunday

JULY

7 Monday

8 Tuesday   LILIAN BELLAMY BORN 1947

9 Wednesday

10 Thursday   *First Quarter*

11 Friday   DORIS ARCHER BORN 1900

12 Saturday

13 Sunday

JULY

14 Monday   Holiday, Northern Ireland (Battle of the Boyne)

15 Tuesday   St Swithin's Day

16 Wednesday

17 Thursday

18 Friday   *Full Moon*

19 Saturday   JACK WOOLLEY BORN 1919

20 Sunday   JAMIE PERKS BORN 1995

JULY

21 Monday

22 Tuesday

23 Wednesday

24 Thursday

25 Friday   *Last Quarter*

26 Saturday

27 Sunday

1959 VILLAGE FETE (from left to right) MADAME GAVRONNE (IRENE PRADER), CHARLES GRENVILLE (MICHAEL SHAW), MRS TURVEY (COURTNEY HOPE) AND DAN ARCHER (HARRY OAKES)

JULY | AUGUST

28 Monday

29 Tuesday

30 Wednesday

31 Thursday

1 Friday   *New Moon*

2 Saturday

3 Sunday

AUGUST

4 Monday

Summer Bank Holiday, Scotland and Republic of Ireland
BETTY TUCKER BORN 1950

5 Tuesday

6 Wednesday

7 Thursday

EMMA GRUNDY BORN 1984
MATT CRAWFORD BORN 1947

8 Friday

First Quarter
SHULA HEBDEN-LLOYD AND KENTON ARCHER BORN 1958

9 Saturday

10 Sunday

AUGUST

11 Monday

12 Tuesday

13 Wednesday

14 Thursday

15 Friday

16 Saturday   *Full Moon*

17 Sunday   JULIE PARGETTER-CARMICHAEL BORN 1924

BLACKBERRY & BANANA BRULEE

Ruth's culinary skills have improved over the years and she makes the most of living in the country by using organic local produce whenever she can. Josh and Ben are still of an age to enjoy blackberrying, and the whole family loves Ruth's homemade blackberry and banana brûlée.

Serves 6

INGREDIENTS

6 bananas
Lemon juice
700g (1^1/$_2$lb) blackberries
130g (4^1/$_2$oz) golden caster sugar
300ml (10floz) whipped double cream

METHOD

- Chop the bananas and squeeze lemon juice over them to stop them browning.
- Add the bananas to the blackberries and sprinkle the fruit with 85g (3oz) golden caster sugar.
- Cover with whipped cream and put in the refrigerator until ready to serve, then sprinkle with the remaining caster sugar and brown under a preheated grill.

RUTH'S TOP TIP

Delicious with other seasonal fruits such as raspberries, strawberries and peaches. Freeze them in the summer and you can use them in the winter to remind you that spring is just around the corner!

AUGUST

18 Monday

19 Tuesday

20 Wednesday

21 Thursday

22 Friday

23 Saturday   *Last Quarter*

24 Sunday

25 Monday   Summer Bank Holiday, UK (exc. Scotland)

26 Tuesday

27 Wednesday   EMMA AND WILLIAM GRUNDY MARRIED 2004

28 Thursday

29 Friday

30 Saturday   *New Moon*

31 Sunday

WILLIAM AND EMMA GRUNDY (PHILIP MOLLOY AND FELICITY JONES)

SEPTEMBER

1 Monday

Holiday, Canada (Labour Day) and USA (Labor Day)

2 Tuesday

First Day of Ramadân (subject to sighting of the moon)

3 Wednesday

LILIAN AND RALPH BELLAMY MARRIED 1971

4 Thursday

5 Friday

6 Saturday

7 Sunday

Father's Day, Australia and New Zealand
First Quarter

8 Monday

9 Tuesday

10 Wednesday

11 Thursday   GUY AND CAROLINE PEMBERTON MARRIED 1995

12 Friday

13 Saturday   JOSHUA ARCHER BORN 1997

14 Sunday

SEPTEMBER

15 Monday

Full Moon

---

16 Tuesday

---

17 Wednesday

---

18 Thursday

JOE GRUNDY BORN 1921
DAVID ARCHER BORN 1959

---

19 Friday

---

20 Saturday

---

21 Sunday

SHULA AND MARK HEBDEN MARRIED 1985

SEPTEMBER

22 Monday

Autumnal Equinox
Last Quarter
GRACE ARCHER DIED 1955

23 Tuesday

24 Wednesday

25 Thursday

26 Friday

27 Saturday

28 Sunday

EDWARD GRUNDY BORN 1984

HELEN ARCHER (LOUIZA PATIKAS)

MIKE KELLY

29 Monday

Michaelmas Day
New Moon
ALICE ALDRIDGE BORN 1988
ELIZABETH AND NIGEL PARGETTER MARRIED 1994

30 Tuesday

Jewish New Year (Rosh Hashanah)
KATE MADIKANE BORN 1977

1 Wednesday

OMNIBUS FIRST HEARD ON RADIO 4 1967

2 Thursday

GODFREY BASELY, CREATOR OF *THE ARCHERS*, BORN 1904
FIRST DAILY EPISODES ON RADIO 4 1967

3 Friday

JILL ARCHER BORN 1930

4 Saturday

5 Sunday

OCTOBER

6 Monday

7 Tuesday   *First Quarter*

8 Wednesday

9 Thursday   Jewish Day of Atonement (Yom Kippur)

10 Friday   SUSAN CARTER BORN 1963

11 Saturday

12 Sunday

13 Monday

Holiday, Canada (Thanksgiving Day)
Holiday, USA (Columbus Day)

14 Tuesday

Jewish Festival of Tabernacles (Succoth), First Day
Full Moon

15 Wednesday

16 Thursday

17 Friday

18 Saturday

ARCHERS ADDICTS FOUNDED 1990

19 Sunday

20 Monday

21 Tuesday

Jewish Festival of Tabernacles (Succoth), Eighth Day
Last Quarter

22 Wednesday

23 Thursday

24 Friday

United Nations Day
GEORGE BARFORD BORN 1928
FIRST EPISODE FROM THE MAILBOX BROADCAST 2004

25 Saturday

26 Sunday

British Summertime ends

ADAM MACY (ANDREW WINCOTT) AND IAN CRAIG (STEPHEN KENNEDY)

LUCAS NORTH

27 Monday

Holiday, Republic of Ireland
Holiday, New Zealand (Labour Day)
DORIS ARCHER DIED 1980

28 Tuesday

New Moon

29 Wednesday

30 Thursday

31 Friday

Hallowe'en

1 Saturday

All Saints' Day

2 Sunday

HOME FARM

Farm Facts

Home Farm consists of 1585 acres of mainly arable land, with 80 acres of woodland, 4 acres of strawberries, a 25-acre riding course, fishing lake and "maize maze".

The Aldridges have a complex family tree, Jennifer has four children by three different men! Daughter Kate has lost no time in following in her mother's footsteps; Phoebe, Kate's first child, lives with her father Roy Tucker in Ambridge, while Kate is in Johannesburg with husband Lucas Madikane and her two children. Meanwhile, Brian Aldridge has had several affairs, finally sowing his oats with local doctor's wife Siobhan Hathaway and fathering his first and only son Ruairi. Siobhan moved to Germany and somehow the Aldridge family managed to stay together. Recently events took a dramatic turn, bringing in their wake an unlooked for challenge for Brian and Jennifer, testing their feelings for each other to the limit.

- In 1994, Nelson Gabriel offered Debbie a partnership in his antiques business, but she turned him down, finding the draw of Home Farm too strong to ignore.

- Archers fan sites use colourful shorthand to describe characters. Allrich is Aldridge (surprise, surprise!). Nintendo is Noluthando and Furbie is Phoebe. Chisduffer for Christopher Carter made us smile but our favourite just has to be Dilbert for Robert Snell.

- Kate's secret ingredient in a special dish prepared for her parents made them very happy. It was cannabis!

- Actors have a life outside Ambridge. As well as Debbie, actress Tamsin Greig plays frustrated Fran Katzenjammer in Channel 4's comedy classic *Black Books*, as well as love-lorn Dr Caroline Todd in *Green Wing*.

 Sizzling Storylines

- Siobhan was not Brian's first swerving step from the sanctity of marriage... in 1985 he had a fling with Ambridge aristocrat Caroline. When Jennifer found out what was going on she nearly chased Caroline out of town but, luckily for Oliver Sterling, she stuck around until the gossip died down.

- Debbie came to the family's rescue after her natural father, Roger Travers-Macy burst back into her life on her 21st birthday. After starting an affair with Jennifer, Roger was seen off by Debbie who could not tolerate the tension infecting the farm.

- 2006 witnessed a landmark moment when Ian proposed to Adam over a romantic dinner for two, and a few weeks later Ambridge saw its first civil partnership.

NOVEMBER

3 Monday

4 Tuesday

5 Wednesday

Guy Fawkes' Day

6 Thursday

First Quarter

7 Friday

JULIA CARMICHAEL-PARGETTER DIED 2005
15,000TH EPISODE BROADCAST 2006

8 Saturday

9 Sunday

Remembrance Sunday, UK

DAVID AND RUTH ARCHER (TIMOTHY BENTINCK AND FELICITY FINCH)
AND SAM BATTON (ROBIN PIRONGS)

GILES PARK

10 Monday

---

11 Tuesday

Holiday, Canada (Remembrance Day) and USA (Veterans' Day)

---

12 Wednesday

---

13 Thursday

Full Moon
PEGGY WOOLLEY BORN 1924

---

14 Friday

DANIEL HEBDEN-LLOYD BORN 1994
RUAIRI DONOVAN BORN 2002

---

15 Saturday

---

16 Sunday

JILL AND PHIL ARCHER MARRIED 1957

NOVEMBER

17 Monday

18 Tuesday

19 Wednesday

Last Quarter
THE ARCHERS FIRST BROADCAST ON THE INTERNET 1999

20 Thursday

BRIAN ALDRIDGE BORN 1943

21 Friday

CLARRIE AND EDDIE GRUNDY MARRIED 1981

22 Saturday

23 Sunday

NOVEMBER

24 Monday

25 Tuesday

26 Wednesday

27 Thursday

Holiday, USA (Thanksgiving Day)
New Moon

28 Friday

29 Saturday

30 Sunday

Advent Sunday
St Andrew's Day

DECEMBER

WEEK 49
2008

1 Monday

MIKE TUCKER BORN 1949

2 Tuesday

3 Wednesday

4 Thursday

5 Friday

First Quarter

6 Saturday

7 Sunday

DECEMBER

8 Monday

9 Tuesday

10 Wednesday

11 Thursday

12 Friday

Full Moon
LUCY GEMMELL BORN 1971
PAT AND TONY ARCHER MARRIED 1974
LILY AND FREDDIE PARGETTER BORN 1999

13 Saturday

14 Sunday

ADAM MACY AND IAN CRAIG CIVIL PARTNERSHIP 2006

DECEMBER

15 Monday

RUTH AND DAVID ARCHER MARRIED 1988

16 Tuesday

BETTY TUCKER DIED 2005

17 Wednesday

DAN AND DORIS ARCHER MARRIED 1921

18 Thursday

19 Friday

Last Quarter

20 Saturday

21 Sunday

Winter Solstice
CHRISTINE BARFORD BORN 1931

HOT & SPICY PUNCH

Jennifer's parties are celebrated throughout Ambridge and her guests always enjoy her generous hospitality. Christmas at Home Farm wouldn't be the same without a seasonal punch to get the party going, and it's the one time Brian lends a hand with the preparations.

Makes 24 glasses

INGREDIENTS

150g (5oz) sugar
6 oranges
24 cloves
3 level teaspoons ground nutmeg
3 sticks cinnamon
200ml (7fl oz) water
5 lemons
3 x 500ml bottles (3 x 8fl oz) cider
300ml (10fl oz) rum
300ml (10fl oz) brandy

METHOD

- Remove the zest from 3 oranges and halve and juice them.
- Put the juice, sugar and zest into a large pan.
- Cut the remaining oranges into eight sections, put a clove into the peel of each section. Add to the pan with the nutmeg.
- Peel the lemons using a potato peeler, and add the peel to the pan with the water and cinnamon.
- Heat gently until the sugar dissolves, then simmer for 5 minutes. Leave to cool until needed.
- A few minutes before you are ready to serve, remove the cinnamon sticks. Add the rum and brandy, and re-heat the punch for a couple of minutes. The punch is now ready to serve.

BRIAN'S TOP TIP

Lilian likes her drinks served with style and Brian aims to please (anything for a quiet life!)... To make the glasses sparkle like frost on a Christmas morning, soak the rim of each glass in the leftover lemon juice and dip into a plate of caster sugar to coat.

22 Monday

Jewish Festival of Chanukah, First Day

23 Tuesday

24 Wednesday

Christmas Eve
DEBBIE ALDRIDGE BORN 1970
SHULA AND ALISTAIR LLOYD MARRIED 1998

25 Thursday

Christmas Day
Holiday, UK, Republic of Ireland, Canada,
USA, Australia and New Zealand

26 Friday

Boxing Day (St Stephen's Day)
Holiday, UK, Republic of Ireland,
Canada, Australia and New Zealand

27 Saturday

New Moon

28 Sunday

GODFREY BASELY PRESENTED *INTRODUCING THE ARCHERS* 1950

29 Monday

Islamic New Year (subject to sighting of the moon)

30 Tuesday

31 Wednesday

New Year's Eve
JOHN ARCHER BORN 1975

1 Thursday

New Year's Day
Holiday, UK, Republic of Ireland, Canada,
USA, Australia and New Zealand
JACK AND PEGGY WOOLLEY MARRIED 1991
THE ARCHERS FIRST BROADCAST NATIONWIDE 1951

2 Friday

Holiday, Scotland and New Zealand

3 Saturday

4 Sunday

First Quarter

From left to right NED LARKIN (BILL PAYNE), TOM FORREST (BOB ARNOLD), JACK ARCHER (DENIS FOLWELL), DORIS ARCHER (GWEN BERRYMAN), DAN ARCHER (MONTE CRICK), CAROL GRENVILLE (ANNE CULLEN), PHILIP ARCHER (NORMAN PAINTING) AND WALTER GABRIEL (CHRIS GITTINS)

NOTES

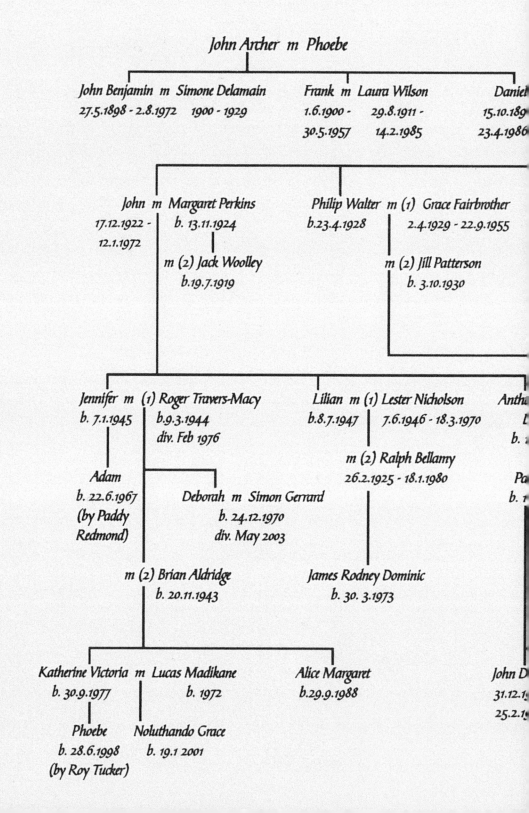

John Archer m Phoebe

John Benjamin m Simone Delamain
27.5.1898 - 2.8.1972   1900 - 1929

Frank m Laura Wilson
1.6.1900 -   29.8.1911 -
30.5.1957   14.2.1985

Daniel
15.10.189
23.4.1986

John m Margaret Perkins
17.12.1922 -   b. 13.11.1924
12.1.1972

m (2) Jack Woolley
b.19.7.1919

Philip Walter m (1) Grace Fairbrother
b.23.4.1928   2.4.1929 - 22.9.1955

m (2) Jill Patterson
b. 3.10.1930

Jennifer m (1) Roger Travers-Macy
b. 7.1.1945   b.9.3.1944
div. Feb 1976

Adam
b. 22.6.1967
(by Paddy
Redmond)

Deborah m Simon Gerrard
b. 24.12.1970
div. May 2003

m (2) Brian Aldridge
b. 20.11.1943

Lilian m (1) Lester Nicholson
b.8.7.1947   7.6.1946 - 18.3.1970

m (2) Ralph Bellamy
26.2.1925 - 18.1.1980

James Rodney Dominic
b. 30. 3.1973

Antho
b.

Pa
b.

Katherine Victoria m Lucas Madikane
b. 30.9.1977   b. 1972

Alice Margaret
b.29.9.1988

John D
31.12.1
25.2.1

Phoebe
b. 28.6.1998
(by Roy Tucker)

Noluthando Grace
b. 19.1 2001